ICNC **SPECIAL REPORT** SERIES

Working Tirelessly for Peace and Equality

Civil Resistance and Peacebuilding in Liberia

Janel B. Galvanek
James Suah Shilue

Table of Contents

Abstract 1

Introduction 3

I. An Integrated Framework for Civil Resistance and Peacebuilding 5

II. Latent Conflict in Liberia (Before 1980) 7
    A. The Unique Founding of Liberia and the History of Oppression 7
    B. Strategies to Ensure Equal Rights 8
    C. Impact of Strategies and Outlook for the Future 9

III. Overt Conflict (1980 – 2003) 11
    A. Dictatorship and Civil War 11
    B. Strategies to End the Violence 12
        1. Encouraging Dialogue 13
        2. Civil Resistance Strategies 15
            Documentation and the Demand for Accountability 15
            Disruptive Collective Actions 17
            Women Spearheading Civil Resistance 18
    C. Impact of Peacebuilding and Civil Resistance Strategies During the War 20
    D. Strategic Complementarity in Order to End the War 22

IV. Conflict Settlement (2003) 24
    A. Civil Resistance During the Negotiations 24
    B. Impact of the Ongoing Resistance to War 26

V. Post-Settlement: After the Peace Accord 27
    A. Transitioning to Peace 27
    B. Changing the Focus of Peacebuilding 28
    C. Civil Resistance During the Post-Settlement Phase 29
    D. Impact of Civil Resistance and Peacebuilding 30

Conclusion 32

Cited Bibliography 34

About the Authors 36

Tables

TABLE 1: **Dynamics of civil resistance and peacebuilding** 4

TABLE 2: **Dudouet's civil resistance and peacebuilding strategies and impacts** 5

ABSTRACT

FROM THE ESTABLISHMENT of the Liberian state in 1847, the Americo-Liberian settlers—descendants of freed slaves from the United States—imposed indirect rule over the majority indigenous Liberian population that was oppressive, marginalizing and exploitative. This treatment of the native population became increasingly unsustainable, and in 1980 the settler government was overthrown. The first indigenous Liberian took over political leadership for the first time since 1847. But instead of uniting Liberians as was widely expected, a 10-year dictatorship emerged, followed by a brutal civil war that lasted until 2003. Many organizations were actively working for peace and advocating for democratic change throughout the civil war, most notably the Inter-Religious Council of Liberia, the Mano River Women's Peace Network, and the Catholic Justice and Peace Commission. Although these organizations carried out various activities in the pursuit of peace and facilitated regular consultations with the warring parties, peace remained elusive for Liberia until 2003. At this time, the Mass Action for Peace, a civil resistance campaign led by the Women in Peacebuilding Network began organizing protests, sit-ins, and a 2-month vigil outside the building where the peace negotiations were being held, actively pressuring the sides to come to an agreement.

> *Many different actors in Liberia pursued strategies of peacebuilding and civil resistance simultaneously, which led to the complementarity of their work and increased the impact they had on the peace process, as well as political and civic reform.*

Using the framework developed by Véronique Dudouet in her 2017 ICNC Special Report, *Powering to Peace: Integrated Civil Resistance and Peacebuilding Strategies*, we examine the methodologies and approaches of the various actors involved in civil resistance and peacebuilding throughout each phase of conflict in Liberia, from a period of latent conflict (before 1980) to the post-settlement phase after 2003. Many different actors in Liberia pursued strategies of peacebuilding and civil resistance simultaneously, which led to the complementarity of their work and increased the impact they had on the peace process, as well as political and civic reform. This case study takes an in-depth look at the interaction of these strategies in their common pursuit of peace and justice in Liberia.

"Peace is the best that you can have; it cuts across class and region. When at peace, everything is possible. ...The message of peace transcends all other barriers, even religion and tribes."[1]

Introduction

WITHIN MANY VIOLENT CONFLICTS, there are forces striving for peace. These forces are comprised of actors using differing approaches with the same objective—the end of violence. All actors use the means available to them to work for change. Yet sometimes these different approaches seem a world apart. For instance, peaceful protesters demonstrating through the streets proclaiming their demands seem unrelated to the calm determination of religious leaders as they reach out to and negotiate with parties involved in the conflict. Each approach has an essential role to play. Indeed, the complementarity of these approaches can help affect substantive change. Furthermore, a single actor can employ both approaches, based on the current need, blurring the distinction between the two. Such can be the case of civil resistance and peacebuilding activities in general and, specifically, in Liberia—strikingly different, yet collaborative and complementary.

Civil resistance is defined by Kurt Schock as the "sustained use of methods of nonviolent action by civilians engaged in asymmetric conflicts with opponents not averse to using violence...."[2] Gene Sharp organized all methods of resistance into three categories: 1) protest and persuasion (such as formal declarations, protests and vigils); 2) non-cooperation (such as stay-at-home actions, boycotts and strikes); and 3) nonviolent intervention (such as fasts or sit-ins).[3] Peacebuilding in turn can be described as "all activities aimed at promoting peace and overcoming violence in a society"[4] and uses decidedly different methods for achieving its goals, such as dialogue and negotiation.

We investigate the various civil resistance and peacebuilding strategies employed in Liberia preceding, during, and following the civil war in the 1990s until 2003. When the Liberian state was established in 1847, the Americo-Liberian settlers imposed a form of indirect rule that oppressed, marginalized and exploited the native population. Despite the efforts of individuals and organizations to encourage reform of the political and economic systems,

---

1   Interview with Rev. Bartholomew Bioh Colley, February 6, 2019.

2   Kurt Schock, "The Practice and Study of Civil Resistance," *Journal of Peace Research* 50, no. 3 (2013): 277.

3   Gene Sharp, *The Politics of Nonviolent Action* (3 Vols.) (Boston: Porter Sargent, 1973).

4   Berghof Foundation, *Berghof Glossary on Conflict Transformation: 20 Notions for Theory and Practice*, 62.

this oppression remained in place until the settler government was overthrown in 1980. Following a 10-year dictatorship, civil war continued until 2003. Civic engagement was severely restricted during these years, but despite the repression, many organizations continued advocating for peace and democratic change. Throughout the phases of the conflict, these groups employed various civil resistance and peacebuilding strategies. This case study demonstrates that these strategies were not only complementary but were at times overlapping and difficult to distinguish. Furthermore, it reveals that some actors chose peacebuilding and civil resistance methods strategically depending on what would be most effective to meet the need of any given situation.

TABLE 1: Dynamics of civil resistance and peacebuilding across four stages of conflict in Liberia

	LATENT CONFLICT (BEFORE 1980)	**OVERT CONFLICT (1980–2003)**	**CONFLICT SETTLEMENT (JUNE–AUGUST 2003)**	**POST-SETTLEMENT (2003–PRESENT)**
Features of Conflict	133 years of Americo-Liberian hegemony—one party rule.	Military rule/dictatorship of Samuel Doe (1980–1989); two phases of open war: factional rule, failed state, armed rebel groups; and significant violence (1989–2003).	Negotiations leading to peace agreement in Accra.	DDR process; post-war reconstruction and recovery; democratization; overall peaceful environment.
Civil Resistance (CR) Strategies	Overlap with PB strategies at the time: Movement for Justice in Africa (MOJA) and the Progressive Alliance of Liberia (PAL) mobilized civil society and agitated for civil liberties of the indigenous population and political reforms.	Stay-at-home actions; student protests; Women in Peacebuilding Network (WIPNET) and Mass Action for Peace organized sit-ins and protests to force the parties to negotiate; Catholic Justice and Peace Commission (JPC) documented human rights abuses, periodically going underground to continue their work.	Mass Action for Peace held 2-month vigil outside the negotiation venue.	Various trade union and student group activities in response to government strategy and policy.
Peacebuilding (PB) Strategies	Overlap with CR strategies at the time; Albert Porte—crusader for civil liberties.	Inter-Religious Council of Liberia (IRCL) and Mano River Union Women Peace Network sought dialogue and organized meetings between conflict parties.	The peace negotiations between conflict parties.	Women in Peacebuilding Network (WIPNET) activities—DDR support, encouraging women's participation in politics.
Impact	Complementary approaches with significant overlap; joint pressure hastened demise of settler regime.	Empowerment of women activists; agreement of warring parties to meet and talk; interconnectedness of activists in Mano River Basin region.	Complementary CR and PB strategies brought about ultimate settlement.	Environment that allows CR activities demonstrates the success of post-war Liberia and the PB phase.

I. An Integrated Framework for Civil Resistance and Peacebuilding

This case study on Liberia utilizes the framework developed by Véronique Dudouet in her report *Powering to Peace: Integrated Civil Resistance and Peacebuilding Strategies.*[5] This framework (as reproduced in Table 2) demonstrates how these two different approaches can complement each other both conceptually, in order to fully understand the complexity of conflict transformation, and practically, in order to transform real conflicts. In order to achieve just peace, both sets of strategies should be employed.

TABLE 2: Dudouet's civil resistance and peacebuilding strategies and impacts during the four stages of conflict transformation

	LATENT CONFLICT	OVERT CONFLICT	CONFLICT SETTLEMENT	POST-SETTLEMENT
Features of Conflict Phase	Structural violence Low awareness of conflict Power imbalance	Conflict intensification	Conflict and resistance substituted by dialogue of equals	Peace implementation and consolidation
Civil Resistance Strategies	Community organizing/mobilization Violence prevention	Nonviolent action (protest and persuasion, non-cooperation, disruptive and constructive resistance)	Popular pressure at the negotiation table for equitable bargaining outcomes	Nonviolent campaigns for full implementation of just peace
Peacebuilding Strategies	Violence prevention (early warning, preventative diplomacy, dialogue)	Peacekeeping dialogue facilitation (inter and intra-party) human rights monitoring	Inter-party conciliation through (direct or mediated) dialogue and negotiation	Institutionalization of negotiation outcomes through political/security socio-economic reforms, reconciliation and transitional justice
Impact	Underdog's awakening to the need for conflict to address grievances and change the status quo	Violence mitigation, empowerment of the underdog	Negotiated agreement	Sustainable peace with justice

While both civil resistance and peacebuilding strategies use peaceful means, they employ different methods. According to Dudouet, civil resistance has a pro-justice stance, combatting oppression and injustice against marginalized groups by primarily using bottom-up methods. Peacebuilding, on the other hand, uses a multi-track approach involving both grassroots actors as well as higher-level decision makers. Furthermore, peacebuilding

---

5 Véronique Dudouet, *Powering to Peace: Integrated Civil Resistance and Peacebuilding Strategies* (Washington, DC: International Center on Nonviolent Conflict, 2017), 11-12.

actors strive to retain their impartiality by not associating themselves with any side in a conflict, while civil resisters adopt clearly defined anti-status quo positions and goals with a potential opponent in mind. Yet despite the conceptual and practical differences, there remain similarities between peacebuilding and civil resistance, most importantly their common objective of peaceful change. Moreover, the different peacebuilding and civil resistance approaches can be complementary and may allow their objectives to be met more effectively if deployed together.

Dudouet's framework (2017), informed directly by Adam Curle (1971), separates asymmetric conflicts into four stages of transformation: latent conflict, overt conflict, conflict settlement, and post-settlement. Dudouet argues that complementary strategies of peacebuilding and civil resistance can be "applied sequentially or simultaneously at various stages of transformation of asymmetric conflicts, to initiate and support constructive change towards just peace."[6] In the latent conflict stage, peacebuilding strategies can be ineffective in calling for justice and equality for oppressed groups, as their methods are often too conciliatory. Thus, methods of civil resistance are often more effective at developing political awareness and working for equity. During the overt conflict stage, underlying tensions have now broken through the surface. In this stage, both peacebuilding and civil resistance strategies aim to reduce the violence; peacebuilding through methods such as monitoring, advocacy, and dialogue facilitation, and civil resistance through more confrontational methods aimed at ending acute violence and oppression.

In stage three, or the conflict settlement stage, civil resistance strategies can increase the legitimacy of the (traditionally) weaker party and foster more inclusive conflict settlement by encouraging civil participation. Simultaneously, dialogue and third-party mediation are examples of peacebuilding methods that can articulate the needs and interests of all parties into a mutually acceptable solution. The fourth stage of sustainable peace, the post-settlement stage, is reached when the conflict parties have established healthy power relations. Both peacebuilding and civil resistance strategies are essential in this stage in order to help post-conflict societies sustain positive peace; because civil resistance is often linked with grassroots empowerment, it supports and encourages the process of participatory democracy. Peacebuilders can then take the principles and practices derived from civil resistance and incorporate them into the new or reformed institutions and infrastructures of a peaceful society and state. Overall, peacebuilding and civil resistance offer compatible strategies toward shared goals, such as regime change or ending violence. The complementarity of these approaches and how they can work together successfully will be demonstrated through this case study on Liberia.

---

6   Ibid., 18.

II. Latent Conflict in Liberia (Before 1980)

A. The Unique Founding of Liberia and the History of Oppression

Liberia was settled in 1821 by freed slaves from the United States who crossed the Atlantic Ocean in order to live as free men and women on the African continent. This resettlement was facilitated by a philanthropic organization called the American Colonization Society (ACS) which was involved in bringing a halt to the slave trade and repatriating former slaves. Liberia was founded in 1847—making it Africa's first independent republic—primarily as an attempt to keep the colonial powers of Great Britain and France from encroaching on Liberian territory. Yet the indirect rule that the settler population, or Americo-Liberians, as they came to be known, imposed over the indigenous population of the territory greatly resembled colonialism itself,[7] with subordination of the tribal populations in the interior of the country. Thus the settlers monopolized political power and opportunities for higher education, while the indigenous population suffered from marginalization, oppression and severe exploitation. Emmanuel T. Dolo argues that such a "separatist strategy,"—in which the settlers positioned their culture and language as superior to the indigenous culture, and built the necessary social, cultural and economic structures to oppress and marginalize the indigenous population—set the two groups in permanent opposition to each other.[8] This oppressive treatment, which one commentator described as "Black imperialism,"[9] continued throughout the twentieth century and became increasingly unsustainable.

During the years of the William Tubman administration (1944-1971), there were some improvements in suffrage and educational opportunities for indigenous peoples and the settler population of Liberia enjoyed a period of general prosperity.[10] However, President Tubman developed a patronage system based on personal loyalty to him and the cooptation of traditional tribal chiefs.[11] He abolished presidential term limits, established a fearsome security network, and increased the graft and repression by appropriating public funds.[12]

---

7   Stephen Ellis, *The Destruction of Liberia and the Religious Dimension of an African Civil War*, 2nd edition, (New York: New York University Press, 2006), 42.

8   Emmanuel T. Dolo, *Ethnic Tensions in Liberia's National Identity Crisis: Problems and Possibilities* (Cherry Hill, NJ: Africana Homestead Legacy Publishers, 2007), 5-6.

9   M. B. Akpan, "Black Imperialism: Americo-Liberian Rule over the African Peoples of Liberia, 1841-1964," *Canadian Journal of African Studies / Revue Canadienne des Études Africaines* 7, no. 2 (1973): 217-236.

10 Ibid., 23.

11 Amos Sawyer, *Beyond Plunder: Toward Democratic Governance in Liberia* (Boulder: Lynne Rienner Publishers, 2005), 16.

12 Bill Berkeley, *The Graves Are Not Yet Full: Race, Tribe and Power in the Heart of Africa* (New York: Basic Books, 2001), 29-30.

After the death of Tubman, President William R. Tolbert established a more liberal political environment that allowed the voices of the indigenous population to be heard, and a general expansion of civil liberties took place. Nevertheless, the system of structural oppression persisted.[13] President Tolbert tried in vain to manage increasing discontent, not just from within the indigenous communities but also from the new generation of educated elite within the settler community.[14]

B. Strategies to Ensure Equal Rights

Due to the nature of the conflict during the latent phase (up until the military overthrow of the Americo-Liberian government in 1980), it is difficult to strictly classify the societal actions as either civil resistance or peacebuilding. Much of the activism throughout this time was aimed at persuading the government to change policies that marginalized the native people. To this end, activists used different strategies depending on the situation.

One prominent crusader for civil liberties and press freedom during the 1960s and 1970s was Albert Porte. Porte was a teacher and social commentator who regularly wrote pamphlets criticizing government corruption and the excessive authority of the presidency. Prior to the violent coup in 1980, Porte sensed the anarchy the country was heading into, and thus dedicated his life to advocating for change in governance by questioning the violations that he observed. In his defense of civil liberties, he was critical of both the Tubman and Tolbert administrations, and his activism inspired many indigenous Liberians. Throughout his political activism, he never resorted to violence but always pursued a nonviolent campaign for change. Many observers agree that Albert Porte served as the inspiration for many social groups and influenced practices of civil resistance in Liberia.

Two of the prominent activist groups that emerged during the settlers' rule were the Movement for Justice in Africa (MOJA) and the Progressive Alliance of Liberia (PAL). Although they differed in their ideological underpinnings, methods, and aims, the two movements represented the interests of the majority indigenous population that was systematically excluded from the social, economic and political governance processes in Liberia. MOJA was a social movement organized in 1973 by a group of students and professors at the University of Liberia, including Amos Sawyer, Togba-Nah Tipoteh and Boima Fahnbulleh. The movement was initially founded to educate the public about the liberation wars in Africa and to mobilize material support. But as MOJA's membership expanded, it took on domestic issues such as civil liberties, equal opportunity, and poverty. PAL was

---

13   Dolo, 25-29.

14   Martin Meredith, *The State of Africa: A History of Fifty Years of Independence* (London: Simon & Shuster UK Ltd, 2005), 547.

originally founded by G. Baccus Matthews for Liberians in the United States. When it opened its office in Monrovia in 1978, it quickly found its main base of support among the unemployed and under-employed of urban Liberia.

Together, MOJA and PAL—supported by other professional organizations, interest groups and student bodies—mobilized civil society, agitated for political reforms and made demands on the state. In the early stages of their campaigns against the Americo-Liberian oligarchy, the activists of MOJA and PAL introduced revolutionary slogans like "No more sleeping, our eyes are opened" and "In the cause of the people, the struggle continues." These slogans cultivated a sense of commonality and identity that helped to distinguish the privileged class from the underprivileged masses. MOJA also created Susukuu, a socio-economic advisory service that had both economic and ideological motives. Through their unique dress code and by creating a common identity, they became a symbol for the oppressed masses.

Together, MOJA and PAL—supported by other professional organizations, interest groups and student bodies—mobilized civil society, agitated for political reforms and made demands on the state.

C. Impact of Strategies and Outlook for the Future

The situation in Liberia before 1980 adequately reflects Dudouet's description of latent conflict in that structural violence and underlying societal injustices and tensions had not yet spilled over into overt conflict. Although relations between the social groups were unbalanced and tense,[15] there still remained a lack of awareness among the settlers that the indigenous population was being treated unjustly, and the oppressed had only slowly begun to resist in a more organized and collective fashion. According to Jeremy Levitt, MOJA and PAL began working together to pressure the government to make fundamental changes to the way resources were allocated and poor, rural, and unemployed Liberians were kept at the periphery of decision making.[16] In the increasingly charged atmosphere, the administration's attempts to dramatically raise the price of rice—Liberia's staple food—provoked PAL to lead the Rice Riot protest on April 14, 1979, with thousands of Liberians marching on the Executive Mansion, fifty of whom died at the hands of the police.

The collective actions and advocacy of PAL, MOJA, and other organizations during this latent conflict stage had a number of positive effects, including increasing the settler population's awareness of the pervasive inequality in the country and encouraging Liberians to

---

15   Dudouet, 19.

16   Jeremy I. Levitt, *The Evolution of Deadly Conflict in Liberia: From 'Paternaltarianism' to State Collapse*, 2005, 17-18.

demand political reform. Their civil resistance methods provided the means for the "underdogs to develop their own political awareness ... and to bring their acute collective grievances into the public realm."[17] Liberians were, however, unable to harness this nonviolent action and scale it into a larger movement against inequality and marginalization. Instead, the price increase of rice and the brutal police response to the protest led to even greater violence. A year later, the Tolbert administration was violently removed by the military, setting the stage for a civil war.

---

17   Dudouet, 19.

III. Overt Conflict (1980–2003)

A. Dictatorship and Civil War

President Tolbert and many members of his cabinet were killed in a military coup on April 12, 1980, ending the political domination of the Americo-Liberians and sparking the beginning of a 23-year period of instability, dictatorship and war. The coup leader, Samuel Doe, an indigenous Liberian and sergeant in the military, would go on to rule the country brutally for ten years. Although initially seen as an opportunity for indigenous Liberians to end their oppression, the Doe government had no alternative vision for how the country should be governed following the deposition of the Americo-Liberian regime.[18] The new government was accused of extensive human rights abuses, the overreaching power of the military, and a hegemony that favored Doe's Krahn ethnic group. This led to a dramatic increase in violent animosities between the various indigenous ethnic groups in Liberia that before 1980 were minimal.[19]

In December 1989, Charles Taylor exploited these ethnic tensions and launched his rebellion against the Doe regime, sparking the first phase of the Liberian civil war. Taylor encouraged a climate of violence in which the young rebels of his National Patriotic Front of Liberia (NPFL), seeking revenge for Doe's brutality, terrorized the population and committed atrocities on a massive scale. After Doe's assassination in 1990, an ECOWAS peacekeeping force—deployed to the country as the Economic Community of West African States Monitoring Group (ECOMOG)—attempted to calm the situation in Monrovia and defend the new interim government. But Taylor refused to acknowledge the interim government and attacked the ECOMOG troops. Ultimately, ECOMOG managed to control the capital city while Taylor ruled much of the Liberian interior, "Greater Liberia," which became his personal fief, exploited for its natural resources. The interior was ruled with such arbitrary brutality that by 1992, 40% of the population had sought refuge in the capital.[20] Eventually the 1996 Abuja peace agreement paved the way for presidential elections in July 1997, which Taylor won decisively. His victory has been credited to Liberians' fatigue of war and longing for peace, as Taylor had made it clear prior to the vote that were he not elected, he would resume the war.

Taylor's years as president were marked by further human rights abuses, widespread corruption, arms smuggling, financial support and strategic direction for the Revolutionary United Front (RUF) rebels in Sierra Leone, and the exploitation of the country's resources and

---

18   Sawyer, 2005, 18.

19   James Suah Shilue, "Citizenship or 'Autochthony' in Post-Conflict Liberia?: The Perils and Challenges of Ethnic/Religious Connections Forged by War and History," *Journal of Religion, Conflict and Peace* 5, no. 1 and no. 2, (Fall 2011–Spring 2012).

20   Sawyer, 2005, 25.

citizens. Taylor became an international pariah, with both an arms embargo and trade sanctions imposed on Liberia.[21] The second phase of the Liberian war began shortly after Taylor was elected, with armed groups—specifically Liberians United for Reconciliation and Democracy (LURD) and Movement for Democracy in Liberia (MODEL)—challenging Taylor's autocratic and violent rule. By 2003, Taylor had lost control over much of the country and had been indicted by the United Nations Special Court for Sierra Leone for war crimes. He eventually resigned as president and fled to Nigeria in August 2003. The Comprehensive Peace Agreement (CPA) was signed in Accra shortly thereafter by the government, the armed groups and various political parties.

B. Strategies to End the Violence

During the 10-year repressive rule of Samuel Doe, advocating for human rights or protesting the government was an extremely dangerous undertaking. Press argues that "the Doe regime had a very low tolerance of demonstrations or criticism. The repression that characterized not just the start but the whole of Doe's regime blocked the successful functioning of a vital, nonviolent social movement."[22] All organizations were banned while imprisonment and torture for any social activism were common. Nevertheless, a small group of students, journalists, clergy members and attorneys maintained a "low-level nonviolent resistance" to the regime, at great risk to themselves.[23] Students produced anonymous pamphlets criticizing the government, the *Daily Observer* newspaper continued its honest reporting on the horrific conditions in the country (despite being shut down several times), and the bishops of the United Methodist and Roman Catholic churches spoke out about the human rights abuses.[24]

After Doe's assassination, the repression of civil activism and the risks of speaking out remained. In the chaos of the civil war and the accompanying high level of violence, instead of further withdrawing from public life, many civil society organizations launched their pro-peace work and individuals mobilized to counter violence in the country. These included human rights organizations, women's groups, and religious committees. Collectively, they employed a variety of nonviolent techniques and methods, including both peacebuilding and civil resistance strategies, to advocate for peace and end the war.

---

21 Janel B. Galvanek, *Pragmatism and Mistrust: The Interaction of Dispute Resolution Mechanisms in Liberia* (Berlin: Berghof Foundation, 2016), 12.

22 Robert M. Press, *Ripples of Hope: How Ordinary People Resist Repression Without Violence* (Amsterdam: Amsterdam University Press, 2015), 163.

23 Ibid, 164.

24 Ibid., 165-168.

1. **Encouraging Dialogue**

Dialogue and engagement with armed groups as part of the peacebuilding efforts started shortly after the outbreak of the war, when two major religious institutions—the Liberian Council of Churches and the National Muslim Council of Liberia—established the Interfaith Mediation Committee (IFMC) in 1990.

Religious leaders are well respected in Liberia and religions "wield significant moral authority largely through the services they offer in relief work, health, and education."[25] The religious leaders took advantage of this authority to engage both government actors and rebels directly. The IFMC was a fearless advocate for peaceful settlement and democratic change throughout the war, using dialogue to courageously and repeatedly reach out to the warring parties.

In June 1990, the IFMC presided over the first peace talks between the Armed Forces of Liberia (AFL) and the National Patriotic Front of Liberia (NPFL) in Freetown, Sierra Leone. They negotiated the basic parameters of an agreement between the parties: a ceasefire and security corridor to allow humanitarian aid into the affected areas, a buffer zone, and an international monitoring group. However, before the agreement could be drafted, the NPFL pulled out of the negotiations and returned to Gbarnga.[26] When ECOMOG was established, it adopted the IFMC agreement that had been negotiated in Freetown.[27] It quickly became evident that the NPFL did not respect ECOMOG as a neutral party and perceived them as another faction in the war. Thus, when ECOWAS convened a national conference to appoint an interim government in August 1990, the IFMC was designated as the only neutral organization that could preside over the deliberations.[28]

As the war continued, the IFMC continued its efforts in the search for peace. The religious leaders continued to hold consultations with the armed groups, organized various conferences both at home and abroad, helped set the agenda for meetings, and either convened or were represented at many of the peace negotiations.[29] In 1995, the IFMC became the Inter-Religious Council of Liberia (IRCL), which would continue its engagement with the conflict parties in the later years of the war.

---

25 Woods, 28.

26 Interview with David Kiazolu, former Deputy Secretary General of the Interreligious Council and Emmanuel Bowier, former Liberian Minister of Information. December 7, 2018, Monrovia.

27 Woods, 29, and interview with Emmanuel Bowier.

28 Woods, 29.

29 Max Ahmadu Sesay, "Bringing Peace to Liberia," *An International Review of Peace Initiatives*, (2006), 25.

Another organization active in dialogue and engagement was the Mano River Women's Peace Network (MARWOPNET). In May 2000, women from Sierra Leone and Liberia, including veteran Liberian peace activist Mary Brownell, were invited by ECOWAS to Nigeria. Together with women activists from Guinea, they founded MARWOPNET, a regional peace movement, which was supported by Femmes Afrique Solidarité, an NGO based in Switzerland. Because the three countries share social and ethnic ties, pursuing a regional approach was seen as a potentially effective way of building sustainable peace. Liberia was considered the epicenter for regional instability and, at the peak of the war, many observers assumed that if the Liberian crisis was resolved, peace would return to the Mano River Union region.

> *Liberia was considered the epicenter for regional instability and, at the peak of the war, many observers assumed that if the Liberian crisis was resolved, peace would return to the Mano River Union region.*

Quickly after its founding, the network delivered a women's peace appeal to the Revolutionary United Front (RUF) rebels in Sierra Leone and were invited as delegates to an ECOWAS summit. During the meeting, MARWOPNET representatives addressed regional leaders and emphasized the need to support women's peacemaking programs.[30] Their greatest success was in persuading Charles Taylor and Guinean President Lansana Conté, who had tense relations, to meet. MARWOPNET sent delegations to both Taylor and Conté, who reacted in a similar way to the actions and demands of the women—with initial shock and then grudging respect for their courage. Each leader met with the women's delegation and agreed to their demands to sit with each other and President Kabbah of Sierra Leone.

Mary Brownell was adamant about the meeting, informing President Conté that she would lock the room and sit on the key until the presidents ironed out their differences.[31] The threat of such a creative civil resistance action in support of encouraging dialogue between the warring parties seemed to have worked. Conté eventually consented to the meeting.[32] The three leaders met in Rabat, Morocco, in 2002. However, the women who had made this meeting a reality were excluded from the summit, a "victim of marginalization and a severe shortfall in resources."[33] A few months later, likely due to its advocacy work encouraging dialogue among the warring parties and innovative civil resistance actions, MARWOPNET won delegate status at the 2003 peace talks in Ghana that would ultimately end the war. The

---

30 Michael Fleshman, "African Women Struggle for a Seat at the Peace Table," *Africa Renewal*, 2003.

31 "Liberia: Mother Mary Brownell, Renowned Liberian Civil Society Activist, Educator, Dies At 88," *Front Page Africa*, March 14, 2017. Available at: **https://allafrica.com/stories/201703140629.html**

32 Fleshman, "African Women."

33 Ibid.

delegation was led by Ruth Sando Perry, former Liberian Head of State, and Theresa Leigh-Sherman, Vice-President of MARWOPNET. That year, in recognition of its achievements, MARWOPNET received the United Nations Prize for Human Rights.

While MARWOPNET was conducting its engagement with the armed groups, the Inter-Religious Council of Liberia was carrying out its own dialogue with the warring factions. Towards the end of the war, David Kiazolu, the former Deputy Secretary General of the IRCL, travelled to Guinea to speak with the chief spokesman of the LURD rebels to encourage him to negotiate with Taylor's government. With the support of the Inter-Religious Council of Guinea, Kiazolu was able to secure a meeting with high-level LURD representatives. At the meeting, he was accused of being Taylor's surrogate and a knife was put to his throat. When Kiazolu asked for time to say his final prayers before he was killed, the LURD representatives recognized his genuine intentions and agreed to discuss the possibility of negotiations with the Liberian government. After several days of discussions, Kiazolu returned to Liberia with a letter from the LURD rebels to Taylor saying that the group was ready to negotiate. In response to his peace efforts, Taylor threw Kiazolu in prison and charged him with high treason.[34] Nevertheless, this began a period of high intensity shuttle diplomacy between Guinea, Liberia and Sierra Leone that was complementary to MARWOPNET's peace advocacy efforts and involved many civil society actors.

2. Civil Resistance Strategies

A significant number of initiatives organized in Liberia during the overt phase of the conflict (1980–2003) that aimed to end the war relied on civil resistance methods.

DOCUMENTATION AND THE DEMAND FOR ACCOUNTABILITY

One important part of civil resistance strategies during the overt conflict phase, driven by the constructive, creative and courageous nonviolent resistance, was a meticulous documentation of violence to hold perpetrators accountable.

Monitoring and documentation of human rights violations in a very repressive context is here included as a civil resistance method because this type of action was in practice a form of civil disobedience. This was a civic defiance of the government's covert or overt pressure on its citizens to

The goal of documenting human rights abuses was not only to collect information, but to seek justice once it would be feasible to do so.

turn a blind eye and do nothing when witnessing state repression. The goal of documenting human rights abuses was not only to collect information, but to seek justice once it would be feasible to do so. As is often the case with civil resistance, this type of action was also designed

---

34   Interview with David Kiazolu, December 7, 2018, Monrovia.

to increase the chances of the exposed violations backfiring on the repressor and, thus, win new allies and sympathizers among the public.[35]

Premier among organizations with a focus on documenting human rights violations and accountability was the Catholic Justice and Peace Commission (JPC), founded in 1991 by Michael Francis, the Archbishop of Monrovia, and human rights activist, Samuel Kofi Woods. The intention was for the JPC to act as the mouthpiece of the Catholic Church and shed light on the human rights situation in the country.[36] The Church wanted to be the voice of the voiceless and to show the perpetrators that they would be held accountable for their crimes.[37] Throughout the war, the JPC meticulously documented and reported the widespread atrocities that were being committed by the various armed groups fighting the war. Each Monday, the organization released a "situation report" that listed statistics and facts about the previous week's violence. With financial assistance from a charity organization in the UK, it started the radio program "Justice and Peace Forum," which included a segment entitled "Voices from the Front Line."[38] This segment allowed the voices of people who were being directly impacted by the violent conflict to be heard by others around the country.

In response to their vocal and direct criticism of the armed groups' actions and their advocacy for peace, the staff members of the JPC earned the ire of the various factions and often worked under difficult conditions. They regularly received threats, forcing them periodically to leave their homes and work underground.[39] Nevertheless, they continued to courageously document and report on the grave human rights abuses taking place out of a dedication to their work and the victims of violence. "We are like a microphone to which many people's stories are being told."[40] The JPC was also instrumental in the coordination of and support to other organizations advocating for peace in Liberia. They provided technical support to the IFMC and helped coordinate national stay-at-home actions. They also helped establish the Human Rights Center—a consortium of different organizations in Liberia working for justice and human rights. But it was the reporting and documentation of the violence in the country for which the JPC became well known and well respected. This specific aspect

---

35 Human rights documentation in different contexts could be seen as a peacebuilding measure. As noted by Dudouet, some scholars list monitoring as part of peacebuilding functions (2017, 20-21). In our study, we understand human rights documentation in a particular context as a form of protest and resistance against silence and impunity in the face of oppression.

36 Interview with Samuel Kofi Woods. December 5, 2018, Monrovia.

37 Interview with J. Augustine Toe, Vice Chairperson of the Liberia Anti-Corruption Commission (LACC) and former National Director of the Justice and Peace Commission. December 7, 2018, Monrovia.

38 Interview with Woods, December 5, 2018, Monrovia.

39 Interviews with both Woods and J. Augustine Toe, December 5 and December 7, respectively.

40 *Backstage: Interview with Samuel Kofi Woods,* available at: **http://www.pbs.org/speaktruthtopower/b_wood.htm**

of the work of the JPC is a clear example of a "declaration by organizations and institutions" on Sharp's list of methods of nonviolent action.[41] Nevertheless, the former national director of the JPC describes the work of the JPC much more broadly, as a "combination of everything—peacebuilding, activism, documentation and advocacy."[42]

DISRUPTIVE COLLECTIVE ACTIONS

Students at the University of Liberia were active in organizing regular protests against the dictatorial Doe regime.[43] As President of Bong County Students Association at the time, Rev. Bartholomew Bioh Colley states that he—like many other student leaders—opposed the government's draconian policies, especially towards students and civil society organizations. This often led to protests and the detention of student leaders. Furthermore, on March 9, 1995, and February 15, 1996, mass stay-at-home actions were staged successfully in Monrovia, thanks to a consortium of approximately 50 organizations, led by the IFMC and including the JPC. The consortium included religious organizations, women's organizations, students' groups and professional bodies. The agenda of this consortium and the main objectives of the stay-at-home actions were, among others, to demand disarmament before elections, "to galvanize civic institutions and reduce the danger of legitimate protest [turning violent],"[44] and to voice the dissatisfaction with agreements that were perceived by many in society as rewarding the warring factions.[45] In August 1995, between the two mass stay-at-home actions that closed down businesses and markets, the Abuja Agreement was signed, establishing a transitional government, securing elections for July 1997, and temporarily bringing peace to Liberia. Immediately after the 1996 stay-at-home action, the IRCL successfully launched a civic disarmament campaign to assist in the disarmament, repatriation and resettlement programs.

> *In August 1995, between the two mass stay-at-home actions, the Abuja Agreement was signed, establishing a transitional government, securing elections for July 1997, and temporarily bringing peace to Liberia.*

---

41   Sharp, 1973.

42   Interview with J. Augustine Toe, December 7, 2018, Monrovia.

43   Interview with Rev. Bartholomew Bioh Colley, former Bong County student leader and current Acting Chairperson of the Independent National Commission on Human Rights, Republic of Liberia, February 6, 2019, Margibi County, Robert International Airport.

44   Woods, 30.

45   Sesay, 25

WOMEN SPEARHEADING CIVIL RESISTANCE

No description of the civil resistance activities in Liberia could be complete without a comprehensive overview of the hugely significant role of women. The war in Liberia had been marked by extremely high levels of brutal violence, specifically against women, who were targeted for rape as a weapon of war and had watched their children be taken from them. The violence was so pervasive that some women felt that they had no choice but to become peace activists. These women advocated for women's rights and assisted female war victims, but also fought to make their voices heard in the decision-making processes in the Mano River countries, specifically with regard to pursuing peace. Irrespective of religious persuasion and the precarious security situation in the country, Liberian women established the Liberian Women's Initiative (LWI) in 1994, founded and led by Mary Brownell, which held demonstrations and presented position statements to ECOWAS and faction leaders. The organization was instrumental in drawing attention to the plight of women, communicating the views of women to national and international mediators, and representing women in local, national and international peace negotiations.[46] As a reaction to the marginalization of women from formal peace processes and NGO initiatives, the West African Network for Peacebuilding (WANEP) consulted with women's organizations across the region and launched a regional network called the Women in Peacebuilding Network (WIPNET) in 2001.[47] A core objective of WIPNET was to enable women to transform the helpless victim image that is often ascribed to them in violent conflict and instead promote a more assertive image of women as "stakeholders and active participants in the pursuit of just peace."[48] The Liberian branch of WIPNET was established the following year under the leadership of two church leaders, Comfort Freeman and the future Nobel Peace Prize Laureate, Leymah Gbowee.

By early 2003, as the rebel group LURD was threatening Taylor's hold on Monrovia, the country was tipping into even further chaos and violence which were becoming intolerable for Liberian citizens. WIPNET began Mass Action for Peace, a civil resistance campaign that would see Muslim and Christian women peace activists come together in a powerful and ultimately successful movement for peace. The movement's members organized around their identity as women, irrespective of faith or ethnicity, and emphasized their roles as sisters, mothers, daughters and wives. This allowed them to portray themselves as peaceful and non-threatening, which enabled them to gain a level of access to the conflict parties that may otherwise have been impossible.[49] The objective of Mass Action for Peace was to push the

---

46   Ibid., 26.

47   *Ending Liberia's Second Civil War: Religious Women as Peacemakers* (Berkeley: Berkley Center for Religion, Peace, and World Affairs, 2013), 5.

48   Ibid., 13.

49   Tavaana, *How the Women of Liberia Fought for Peace and Won*, 4.

government and the rebel groups to end the war once and for all. The women did not take sides in the conflict—their only goal was absolute peace. Many women activists and peacebuilders from LWI and MARWOPNET joined the movement, bringing their experience and steadfastness to the campaign.

> *The movement's members organized around their identity as women, and emphasized their roles as sisters, mothers, daughters and wives. This enabled them to gain a level of access to the conflict parties that may otherwise have been impossible.*

The Mass Action for Peace was coordinated by Leymah Gbowee, an activist at St. Peter's Lutheran Church in Monrovia, who eloquently expressed the urgent need for peace and the role that the united women of Liberia should play in its realization. The Liberia Muslim Women for Peace, founded and led by Asatu Bah Kenneth, joined the Mass Action for Peace campaign, which demonstrated the unique interfaith collaboration that underpinned the movement. Wearing the symbolic color white, the women activists from Mass Action for Peace organized large-scale sit-ins and protest assemblies in Monrovia in order to put pressure on the parties to negotiate. They sang and prayed for hours, holding up posters with messages calling for peace. Many of them fasted and others organized a sex strike to pressure their husbands and partners to support peace talks.[50] According to Bah Kenneth, the women divided themselves into various groups, some fasting and others praying, as not all women could fast due to health conditions. The Muslim and Christian women were selected by their respective leaders to form the "prayer warriors," praying, fasting and eating breakfast together. Some members of the campaign were responsible for networking with the warring factions while others were responsible for shuttling women as early as 5:00 a.m. to attend the campaign's events. "When we got to our posted location, we did not speak or communicate verbally with people but just carried posters with peace inscriptions in our hands."[51]

The campaign grew to include thousands of women, attracting international media attention thanks to the support of international NGOs.[52] They presented the campaign's position statements to the Liberian government and to diplomatic missions and UN agencies in the country.[53] One prominent peace activist said "because we were so desperate for peace, I led a delegation of women peace activists to the American embassy to increase visibility and

---

50   Ibid., 5.

51   Interview with Atty. Hon. Asatu Bah Kenneth, Deputy Commissioner General for Naturalization Liberia Immigration Service (LIS) and founding head of Liberia Muslim Women for Peace, January 28, 2019.

52   *Ending Liberia's Second Civil War: Religious Women as Peacemakers* (Berkeley: Berkley Center for Religion, Peace, and World Affairs, 2013), 8.

53   Lisa Schirch and Manjrika Sewak, "The Role of Women in Peacebuilding," Global Partnership for the Prevention of Armed Conflict, 2005, 9.

invoke international attention. We insisted that we would not leave the embassy until the various rebel groups signed the peace agreement."[54] A large group of women congregated daily alongside the main road leading into the city, attracting the attention of bishops and imams who visited to show their support, as well as President Taylor, who would frequently pass by in his motorcade. According to WIPNET activist Vaybah Flomo, the women were even visited by Taylor's deadly Anti-Terrorist Unit, who came to the women's prayer ground and saluted the women they referred to as the 'white head tie women.'[55] The women actively sought an audience with Taylor, and when he granted them a hearing, 2,000 women congregated outside the executive mansion in April 2003.[56] Extracting a promise from Taylor to attend peace talks in Ghana, they then sent a delegation to Sierra Leone, to meet with the LURD leaders who had their headquarters there. Three women, Edwina Sugar Cooper, Grace Jackson and Asatu Bah Kenneth, were appointed to lead the delegation to convince LURD rebels to attend the peace talks in Accra while women lined the streets around the rebels' hotel.[57] Eventually, LURD agreed to attend the talks.

The courage of these women should not be underestimated. Organizing protests and vigils in Liberia at this time was dangerous. Many human rights advocates, journalists and other citizens who spoke up against the violence of the Taylor government were threatened, arrested and even killed. In her acceptance speech for the Nobel Peace Prize, Gbowee states that "we did so because we felt it was our moral duty to stand as mothers and gird our waist, to fight the demons of war in order to protect the lives of our children, their land and their future."[58] Augustine Toe compliments the campaign as a "brave effort by dedicated women," sharing that it was powerful to watch the lengths that these women went to. Although they made themselves vulnerable, they were fearless in their actions.[59]

C. Impact of Peacebuilding and Civil Resistance Strategies During the War

The documentation activities pursued by the Justice and Peace Commission were arguably the most impactful in bringing human rights violations in the country to the attention of the international community. Without the consistent and professional reporting on the massive human rights violations taking place, the international community may have continued to

---

54 Interview with Atty. Hon. Asatu Bah Kenneth, January 28, 2019.

55 Interview with Madam Vaybah Flomo, Head of Christian Women within WIPNET Coalition, February 1, 2019.

56 Tavaana, 10.

57 Interview with Atty. Hon. Asatu Bah Kenneth, January 28, 2019.

58 Leymah Roberta Gbowee, Nobel Lecture, Oslo, December 10, 2011.

59 Interview with Counselor Augustine Toe, December 7, 2018, Monrovia.

ignore the atrocities happening in this small West African country. This documentation showed the scale of violence and convinced the international community to become involved.[60] Kofi Woods even met with President Clinton, which according to him brought a "new level of credibility, visibility, and international legitimacy" to the Liberian cause.[61] Furthermore, the JPC set the standard for accountability in the war. Their mantra—"there can be no peace without justice"—guided their work and created the conditions to hold warlords accountable for their actions. This principle was adhered to throughout the war by different organizations, including the IFMC, who were openly uneasy with allowing peace to be negotiated among warlords at the sake of justice for the victims. They disagreed with the strategy of the international negotiators who sought to accommodate the armed factions with promises of access to state power, believing that such a strategy rewarded crime and perpetuated violence.[62]

> *Without consistent and professional reporting on the massive human rights violations, the international community may have continued to ignore the atrocities happening in this small West African country.*

The IFMC and, afterwards, the IRCL remained true to their principles of dialogue and engagement with all parties throughout the 14 years of armed conflict in Liberia. They retained their neutrality as mediators and trustworthy negotiators, both in the eyes of the factions as well as with the public, all while insisting that violence shouldn't be rewarded with power. Their steadfastness to the cause of dialogue for peace and their courage to seek out engagement despite danger are commendable. The impact of such courage and principled actions is impossible to adequately measure, but they certainly provided Liberians a sense of hope. Liberians knew that their religious leaders were making every effort to reestablish peace in the country. Such determination and courage may have motivated other Liberians to do what they could to end the war. Moreover, Woods argues that the cooperation of prominent Islamic and Christian leaders should not be underestimated for its role in preventing "the emergence of religious disharmony as a component of the civil war."[63]

The impact of the civil resistance campaign, Mass Action for Peace, would become particularly obvious during the peace talks in Ghana in the summer of 2003. Yet the campaign

---

60 Interview with Counselor Toe, December 7, 2018, Monrovia.

61 *Backstage: Interview with Samuel Kofi Woods*, 19--, available at: http://www.pbs.org/speaktruthtopower/b_wood.htm

62 Samuel Kofi Woods II, "Civic Initiatives in the Peace Process," *An International Review of Peace Initiatives, Accord,* (1996).

63 Woods, 32.

had already made an impressive impact in its early stages. First and foremost, it catapulted Liberian women from passive victims to courageous and outspoken advocates for peace. The women activists demanded that the male decision makers in the country listen to their concerns and created a powerful movement that could not be ignored. Arguably, this brave advocacy has directly impacted the increased scope of political roles for women in Liberia since the war.[64] The Mass Action for Peace also had a very positive impact on the relations between Muslim and Christian women. The campaign promoted a "sense of interfaith solidarity" because it united women around their shared experiences in the war rather than dividing them by faith.[65] Many religious leaders supported the campaign, visiting the women during their protests, while the Catholic radio station, Radio Veritas, publicized the campaign's actions.[66] Thus, the Mass Action for Peace had the same profound effect as the Inter-Religious Council of Liberia—emphasizing a common need for peace and a willingness to transgress boundaries to work together.

D. Strategic Complementarity in Order to End the War

Referencing examples in the Philippines and Colombia, Dudouet argues that it is possible to engage effectively in organized nonviolent actions in the midst of armed conflict.[67] This was the case in Liberia, as the conflict actors and dynamics had changed dramatically since the latent conflict phase. Rather than protesting a repressive regime, the civil resistance and peacebuilding actors collaborated to oppose violence and war. The anti-war campaigns actively contributed to peacebuilding. The diverse organizations advocating for peace during Liberia's civil war understood that it was necessary to work together to end the violence. As the initiatives of the organizations varied according to their methods, focus, and target groups, their work proved to be highly complementary. While the IFMC challenged the warlords directly, others worked on the grassroots level and motivated citizens to take a stand against violence. Furthermore, while some international funding was available for the JPC, specifically from IDEA and Miseore in Germany, Woods argues that because there was little donor-driven

---

64 Veronika Fuest, "'This is the Time to Get in Front': Changing Roles and Opportunities for Women in Liberia," *African Affairs* 107, no. 427, (April 2008): 213-214.

65 Berkeley, 7.

66 Tavaana, 4-5.

67 Dudouet, 23.

money to secure, there was little competition among the organizations.[68] This is noteworthy considering Chenoweth and Stephan's argument that "Mobilization among local supporters is a more reliable source of power than the support of external allies...."[69]

The complementarity of the different approaches—civil resistance, direct advocacy and dialogue with armed groups, and the demand for accountability—increased their impact on peace in Liberia since it allowed individuals to use the method in which they were most skilled to secure an end to the violence. There was also significant overlap between these methods, with many organizations employing peacebuilding and civil resistance simultaneously, allowing them to work together and increase their effectiveness, such as with the stay-at-home actions. While the international community often credits the Mass Action for Peace for ending the war in Liberia, in reality various forces came together to foster peace in Liberia, with the Mass Action for Peace being the culmination of many years of dedication and suffering by peace activists. Alaric Tokpa, professor at the University of Liberia and a prominent activist during the war, argues that much of what happened in these prior years laid the groundwork for the initiatives in 2003. "Every little effort by organizations, individuals, agencies, etc., contributed in some way to peace."[70]

---

68 Interview with Woods.

69 Erica Chenoweth and Maria J. Stephan, *Why Civil Resistance Works: The Strategic Logic of Nonviolent Conflict* (New York: Columbia University Press, 2011), 10.

70 Interview with Alaric Tokpa, December 6, 2018, Monrovia.

IV. Conflict Settlement (2003)

Although the Abuja Peace Agreement in 1996 brought temporary peace to the country, it was unfortunately short-lived. Elections were held the following year with extremely high voter turnout, which demonstrated how much Liberians wanted peace. Charles Taylor induced fear in the electorate by openly stating that he would return to war if he didn't win the presidency. His eventual electoral victory was thus a result of people wanting peace, rather than genuine support for him as a candidate. Yet very quickly after the election, the war began again. Liberians were woefully disappointed with the 1996 peace accord and no longer considered it to be relevant. Hence the conflict settlement period in 1996-1997 is not incorporated into the analytical framework and we focus on the 2003 peace talks instead (see Table 1, page 4).

A. Civil Resistance During the Negotiations

In June 2003, peace talks began in Ghana between Charles Taylor's government and the rebel groups, including LURD and MODEL. However, talks broke down when the rebel factions put forth three conditions for halting their onslaught on Monrovia. They demanded that Taylor dissolve his government and step down within ten days of any ceasefire agreement; that a Western-led intervention force should be deployed to monitor the ceasefire, rather than a West African peacekeeping force led by ECOWAS; and that a broad-based government of national unity be put in place, which excluded those who had been indicted by the UN Special Court for Sierra Leone. As the warring factions attempted to reach an acceptable compromise and a peaceful resolution to the conflict, ECOWAS moved in to expedite the creation of an interim government for Liberia.[71] The ECOWAS Standing Mediation Committee convened a conference of all political parties and interest groups for the purpose of establishing a broad-based interim government charged with administering the country and organizing free and fair elections.[72]

A small delegation of women from Mass Action for Peace secured funding to travel to Ghana to follow the negotiations and sustain pressure on the parties to reach an agreement. This delegation was able to mobilize many Liberian refugees in Ghana to take part in civil resistance activities on the sidelines of the negotiations. They made white ribbons to pin on the delegates and began what would be a 2-month vigil in front of the building where the negotiations were taking place. Each day of the negotiations, the delegates were greeted

---

71   Decision A/DEC.2/8/90 of the Community Standing Mediation Committee on the Constitution of an Interim Government in the Republic of Liberia.

72   Ibid.

by women holding posters and signs demanding peace.[73] Simultaneously, the activists of WIPNET continued to release statements emphasizing the civilian casualties of the war and calling for international intervention. They organized a women's forum on the sidelines of the talks in Ghana, where women could discuss and reflect on the progress of the ongoing negotiations. They also continued to meet with the various parties involved in the conflict, including the chief negotiator, General Abdulsalami Alhaji Atiku, a former president of Nigeria.[74] Back home in Liberia, the women of Mass Action for Peace continued their vigils at the Monrovia markets, government offices, and the American and Guinean embassies.[75] Furthermore, the women of WIPNET were invited to attend several negotiation meetings exploring strategies for peace among the armed groups, though they did not have a formal seat at the negotiation table. Still, this was a great success as it demonstrated that Liberian women were stakeholders in the conflict and had a role to play in making peace.[76]

On June 4, 2003, Charles Taylor was indicted by the Special Court for Sierra Leone (SCSL) while he was attending the talks in Ghana and subsequently fled back to Liberia. The talks continued without him and a ceasefire was established between the parties in mid-June, which was met with elation by the women activists. However, the ceasefire barely lasted a week, heavy fighting resumed in and around Monrovia, and the negotiations stalled. The members of Mass Action for Peace became more outspoken and assertive, adopting more aggressive nonviolent tactics. During one of the negotiation sessions, they barricaded the delegates in the room, declaring that no one would be allowed to leave and no food would enter until a message was sent to the fighters in Monrovia to respect the ceasefire. When the men tried to leave the room, the women threatened to strip off their clothes in a disrobing protest and thus bring shame on the men, until the negotiators promised to work towards a comprehensive agreement.[77] The confrontation between the delegates and the women drew the attention of the press which helped to unlock the stalled negotiations, leading to the signing of a peace agreement several weeks later. Charles Taylor resigned as president of Liberia on August 11 and went into exile in Nigeria. The Accra Comprehensive Peace Agreement was signed one week later on August 18, 2003. This was a great success not just for the women of WIPNET and Mass Action for Peace but for all of the individuals and organizations that had worked tirelessly for the cause of peace throughout the years of the war.

---

73 "Ending Liberia's Second Civil War: Religious Women as Peacemakers" (Berkley Center for Religion, Peace, and World Affairs, 2013), 8.

74 Ibid.

75 Tavaana, 5.

76 Berkeley, 9.

77 Tavaana, 5, Schirch and Sewak, 10 and Berkeley, 9.

B. Impact of the Ongoing Resistance to War

In the conflict settlement stage, civil resistance can act as a pre-negotiation strategy because it may accomplish certain tasks that are essential for the settlement process to be effective.[78]

In the conflict settlement stage, civil resistance can act as a pre-negotiation strategy because it may accomplish certain tasks that are essential for the settlement process to be effective.

In this regard, the civil resistance campaign of Mass Action for Peace demonstrated that their demand—a complete end to violence—had the overwhelming support of Liberian society. The women intensified the call for peace such that it was impossible for the conflict parties to ignore them. Moreover, their dedication transformed the concept of peace in Liberia from an outrageous dream to a necessity. The women of Mass Action for Peace who kept up the relentless pressure on the delegates believed that the negotiations had to succeed this time. They refused to disperse until the transition to peace was certain. Building on the years of expertise in peacebuilding and nonviolent resistance actions, the women of Liberia contributed profoundly to ending the war.

Dudouet argues that civil resistance can create inclusive spaces in which to settle a conflict "by empowering a civil society voice demanding participation in the design of post-conflict peacebuilding scenarios."[79] This was the case in Liberia, as the many parties that were witness to the Accra Comprehensive Peace Agreement—including the women's organization MARWOPNET—reflected the diverse and outspoken voices in the post-conflict phase. Fuest credits various elements for the changing roles and opportunities for women in Liberia after the war, including the increased role of women as providers and protectors for their families as well as the emphasis that the international development and peacebuilding agencies placed following the war on women's inclusion in all their programs and activities.[80] Nevertheless, it remains clear that the women's movement at the end of the war and its ultimate success in achieving peace galvanized the women of Liberia to speak up more loudly and participate in political affairs of the country more often and more effectively.

---

78   Dudouet, 23.

79   Ibid., 24.

80   Fuest, 209-10, 218.

V. Post-Settlement: After the Peace Accord
A. Transitioning to Peace

After Taylor's resignation and the signing of the Comprehensive Peace Agreement, a transitional national unity government led the country for two years until national elections were held in 2005. The United Nations Mission in Liberia (UNMIL) officially began on October 1, 2003, and continued until their withdrawal in 2016-2017, during which the country was supported through long-term and extensive international peace-support assistance. Despite tensions during the disarmament, demobilization and reintegration (DDR) process and various election seasons, Liberia has remained peaceful since 2003. Yet the Liberian peace is fragile and has been sustained with extensive international support. The UN-led intervention and the generous support of the donor community have tended to both dwarf and distract from the individual and community-based efforts of ordinary Liberians in navigating the peace process and preventing renewed conflict.

With externally-led peacebuilding approaches, it is arguable that national and community-level endogenous knowledge and efforts have not found effective channels to influence and inform the international decision-making process—despite the theoretical commitment to local ownership in peacebuilding. The real challenge is translating the principle of local ownership into practice in terms of peacebuilding and statebuilding mechanisms, processes, and programs.[81] Unfortunately, the civic actors who helped bring peace to Liberia have not been able to use this momentum and success to develop a clear framework to address social, ethnic and political polarization in the country.

In an attempt to fill important peacebuilding gaps, the Strategic Roadmap for National Healing, Peacebuilding and Reconciliation was formulated in March 2013. The roadmap was intended to foster coherent institutions and systems, to support national healing and reconciliation, and to strengthen efforts towards sustainable peace. The roadmap highlighted some of the problems that Liberian women face, including sexual abuse having been used as an instrument of war. In Liberia's post-war reconstruction process, special attention must be paid to providing women access to economic opportunities and addressing the sexual and gender-based violence (SGBV) that has persisted since the end of the war. Furthermore, women must play key roles in the national reconciliation and peacebuilding processes going forward. Considering the multiplicity of actors in the post-conflict development and peacebuilding processes in Liberia, emphasis has often been placed on the use of conflict-sensitive

---

81   A. Sulleabhain, (2015, IPI) Leveraging Local Knowledge for Peacebuilding and Statebuilding in Africa. Available online at: **http://www.ipinst.org/2015/03/leveraging-local-knowledge-for-peacebuilding-and-statebuilding-in-africa**

approaches to prevent falling into the conflict trap.[82] Current approaches to durable peacebuilding in Liberia should not only focus on the role of international actors, infrastructure, and capacity building, but should also address the extremely high number of Liberians who were displaced during the 14-year civil war.[83]

B. Changing the Focus of Peacebuilding

Many of the organizations that were active in peacebuilding in Liberia have continued their efforts in the post-settlement phase of the conflict, albeit with a slightly altered focus of support for the peacebuilding process. For instance, the women involved in both WIPNET and MARWOPNET carried out activities in support for the DDR process, such as by encouraging combatants to disarm. They also encouraged women's participation in politics by assisting in the voter registration of women prior to the presidential elections of 2005.[84] Furthermore, MARWOPNET has organized youth conferences and worked with market women on issues of conflict resolution, education, and entrepreneurship. Vaybah Flomo, the Head of Christian Women within WIPNET and herself an internally displaced person (IDP) from Lofa County who escaped the horrors of war by fleeing to Monrovia, says that with peace in Liberia, the organization has readjusted its strategy and objectives. The new focus is on empowering women, especially those who were displaced and never returned to their counties of origin, as well as looking after the wellbeing of children. The organization is also fighting to stop SGBV by "doing things to allow children to achieve their own dreams."[85]

During the immediate transition period after the war (2003-2005), the Inter-Religious Council of Liberia took over the watchdog role for the elections, working with political parties and civil society institutions to ensure a free and fair election. Since the end of the war, the Council has primarily concentrated its work on economic issues, good governance and the rule of law, and has continued to use its principled ideology of dialogue with the government's leaders.[86] However, its advocacy on these issues concerning the Johnson-Sirleaf government was limited, leaving many Liberians wondering why the Council has been so inactive. Indeed, the Council is looking for younger leaders to take over the work.[87] Recently, the Council established the

---

82 Peace and conflict literature widely acknowledges that countries that have experienced war often slide back into conflict after 5-10 years of fragile peace, as most of the root causes of the war remain unresolved.

83 James Suah Shilue, and Patricia Fagen, *Liberia: Links Between Peacebuilding, Conflict and Durable Solutions to Displacement,* The Brookings Institution, 2014.

84 Tavaana, 6.

85 Interview with Madam Vaybah Flomo, Head of Christian Women within WIPNET Coalition, February 1, 2019.

86 Interview with David Kiazolu, December 7, 2018.

87 Interview with Rev. Bowier, December 7, 2018.

National Awareness Campaign Committee for the Promotion of Tolerance and Responsible Citizenship in Liberia (NACC) and developed a roadmap to address what it considers to be the most pressing issues: 1) lack of morals and self-discipline in the government; 2) lack of fiscal discipline; 3) lack of spiritual and cultural values; and 4) lack of love and pride of nation.[88]

The Justice and Peace Commission has adjusted well to the post-war dynamics by becoming more involved in civil and legal education while continuing their work in documentation. Through a group of "community justice advisors," the JPC organizes civil education events in rural communities and helps citizens navigate the country's formal and informal justice systems, advising citizens about the costs and implications of the court system and explaining land acquisition laws.[89] The JPC also hosts a call-in radio program that educates people on their legal rights and reaches people in remote areas.[90]

C. Civil Resistance During the Post-Settlement Phase

Although reconstruction and recovery in Liberia has not been easy, there has been no threat of a return to war. The Liberian people eagerly welcomed the UN peacekeeping forces and the massive influx of international engagement in the peacebuilding process. There has been little resistance to the process itself. Instead, civil resistance activity has focused on specific policies of the government that have been perceived as unsatisfactory by citizens. The limited use of civil resistance in post-conflict Liberia should not detract from its usefulness. Trade unions, medical groups and student groups have organized economic shutdowns and strikes in response to various grievances, including the reduction of tariffs and changes in concession agreements. For example, on January 31, 2017, the Patriotic Enterprise of Liberia (PATEL) paralyzed the capital city of Monrovia when they organized and mobilized the business community to close down their businesses until the government listened to their request for a reduction in tariffs on goods and handling fees. There has also been significant contribution to mobilization and advocacy supporting democratic processes and civic engagement, which brings people out onto the streets. Rallies and marches carried out by several Liberian civil society organizations in favor of democratic principles play an important role in raising awareness about the lack of progress that the government is making in ensuring them. That being said, there is much less overlap between peacebuilding and civil resistance in the post-conflict phase, specifically in comparison to the war years. The various initiatives each have their own specific goal, all inherently worthy, but they are more specific and less capable of mobilizing than the call for peace.

---

88   Interview with David Kiazolu, December 7, 2018.

89   Galvanek, 30.

90   Interview with Counselor Toe, December 7, 2018 and Galvanek, 30.

D. Impact of Civil Resistance and Peacebuilding

Many national and international stakeholders have supported Liberia's transition from war to peace. The various contributions, from peacekeeping and statebuilding to development and peacebuilding, have been crucial to ensuring the sustained peace that Liberia is now experiencing. Yet the task of establishing a positive peace in Liberia remains immense, as much of the population struggles daily to make ends meet. While all actors should be commended for their work in keeping and building peace, the needs are overwhelming, and the dire economic situation of the country and its citizens impedes progress towards positive peace.

Nevertheless, the head of Liberian Muslim Women is optimistic and frowns on people expecting everything to become perfect at once. Although the absence of war does not mean absolute peace, she said, "the silence of the guns means a lot, even though we still hear people crying from poverty, wanting help, jobs, etc."[91] She pointed out that her organization is currently preoccupied with capacity building and sustainability for their members, as most of the women came from IDP camps to support the advocacy efforts. Now that peace has returned to Liberia, they need to help these women survive and provide for their children. Indeed, exploring opportunities to enable these women to become self-sufficient could help to prevent abuse and keep some mothers from forcing their young daughters into early marriages.[92]

Rev. Colley shares this perspective. He was involved in the activism of Liberian women and regrets that the women's movement was not able to transform itself politically and economically in order to enable the uneducated women to remain active in politics and become self-sufficient. He feels that their strategy should be included in the national peacebuilding agenda. "These women can play an even greater role in working towards stopping SGBV because they understand the issues. They interacted in the past with the armed groups, who were even dangerous, yet the women spoke to their consciousness and convinced them to disarm." [93]

Nevertheless, one of the greatest achievements of post-settlement phase in Liberia has been the empowerment of women. Much of the peacebuilding work in post-conflict Liberia has helped to "maintain and institutionalize the creative practices and inclusive social

---

91   Interview with Atty. Hon. Asatu Bah Kenneth, Deputy Commissioner General for Naturalization Liberia Immigration, January 28, 2019.

92   Ibid.

93   Interview with Rev. Bartholomew Bioh Colley, former head of Lutheran World Services, Liberia, and current Acting Chairperson Independent National Commission on Human Rights, Republic of Liberia, February 6, 2019, Margibi, County, RIA.

experiments"[94] that were pioneered during the civil resistance campaign of Mass Action for Peace, specifically the inclusion and participation of women. Furthermore, due to the international advocacy for gender mainstreaming and women's rights into the extensive peacebuilding programming rolled out in the country, initiatives in Liberia often target women or at least allow for their substantial inclusion in various activities. Fuest argues that influential women have become much more visible both in the peacebuilding and development sector as well as in local and national government positions.[95]

---

94   Dudouet, 28.

95   Fuest, 217.

Conclusion

Liberia celebrates Fast and Prayer Day on April 12, the anniversary of the coup d'état against the Tolbert regime in 1980, an event that forever reshaped the historical and political dynamics of the country. On this day in 2018, one Liberian journalist lamented that "after 171 years of independence, Liberia is sadly, still classified among the undeveloped countries of the world. Are we better off since 1847? Are we better off since April 14, 1979? Since April 12, 1980? Since December 1989? Are we better off since January 2006? Are we ever going to be?"[96] Indeed, the crisis and war in Liberia left behind a weak state with institutions that are incapable of addressing essential economic and social issues that would benefit the population, resulting in a highly polarized society prone to conflict.

Together, these individuals and organizations, with their different approaches and strategies, were powerful enough to bring international attention to the conflict, force the warring parties to sit at the same table and, ultimately, to end the war.

Nevertheless, Liberians also have a lot that they can be proud of, specifically when one considers the dedicated effort of thousands over the many years of oppression and violent conflict—individuals who worked tirelessly to foster and demand peace from their leaders. These included peacebuilders, protesters, civic organizers, mediators, human rights defenders, dialogue facilitators, advocates for reform, and everyone in between. Together, these individuals and organizations, with their different approaches and strategies, were powerful enough to bring international attention to the conflict, force the warring parties to sit at the same table and, ultimately, to end the war. "Cooperative power arises from the action in concert of people who willingly agree with each other. It flows upward from the consent, support and nonviolent activity of the people."[97]

Unfortunately, many of these significant contributions over the years by civil society in Liberia to end the violence and promote peace have been largely overlooked in the history books. Instead the focus has remained on the role of the various armed actors throughout the years.[98] This oversight continues today, as the focus in recent years has been on security issues, such as the withdrawal of the UN peacekeeping forces. Yet, indigenous Liberian citizens and civil society have played and continue to play an enormous role in supporting

---

96 "Liberia @ 171: Times Have Changed But Things Are Pretty Much the Same," *Front Page Africa*, 2019. Available at: https://frontpageafricaonline.com/letter-from-editor/liberia-171-times-have-changed-but-things-pretty-much-remaining-the-same/

97 Kurt Schock, "Social Movements, Nonviolent," in *The Blackwell Encyclopedia of Sociology*, ed. George Ritzer (Blackwell, Oxford, 2007), 4462.

98 See Sesay (1996).

the ongoing peacebuilding process. In doing so, they resort to various strategies whose overarching feature is their nonviolent character. There is a need to recognize and include these efforts and initiatives in the nation's memory and the international narrative on Liberia.

This report shows how various peacebuilding and civil resistance actions were employed in Liberia before, during and following the civil war in order to advocate for civil liberties, democratic change, justice and peace. These actions often used different methods and strategies but were always complementary in their pursuit for a more just and peaceful Liberian society. While the Dudouet integrated framework for civil resistance and peacebuilding clusters actions into these distinct categories, such an analytical distinction is not always neatly in line with actions on the ground. During the war in Liberia, action-takers did not necessarily make this distinction and blended both approaches in their activism for peace. For them, peace was the ultimate objective and they used whichever nonviolent approach they thought would be most useful for them at the time. Furthermore, even if the framework helps to clearly delineate various phases of conflict and different types of actions present during these phases, the unique impact that the mixing of approaches and the resulting complementarity can have must also be acknowledged. Specifically during the war, this complementarity of strategies and actions increased ordinary people's capacity to affect real change in Liberia. Thus, the Liberian case study enriches the analysis by also challenging, to some extent, neatly defined analytical borders between various methods used to pursue peace and justice in the country.

Today, Liberia continues to suffer from a lack of development, poor governance and a struggling economy. Yet organized violence of any kind has thankfully remained at bay. The peace that Liberia has today—however fragile—can be credited to those individuals and organizations who worked tirelessly throughout the years for peace and equality, with peacebuilding methods, civil resistance methods, or some creative mixture of the two.

The peace that Liberia has today—however fragile—can be credited to those who worked tirelessly for peace and equality, with peacebuilding methods, civil resistance meor some creative mixture of the two.

Cited Bibliography

Akpan, M. B. "Black Imperialism: Americo-Liberian Rule over the African Peoples of Liberia, 1841-1964." *Canadian Journal of African Studies / Revue Canadienne des Études Africaines* 7, no. 2 (1973): 217-236.

Berkeley, Bill. *The Graves Are Not Yet Full: Race, Tribe and Power in the Heart of Africa.* New York: Basic Books, 2001.

Chenoweth, Erica, and Stephan, Maria J. *Why Civil Resistance Works: The Strategic Logic of Nonviolent Conflict.* New York: Columbia University Press, 2011.

Curle, Adam. *Making Peace.* London: Tavistock Pubs, 1971.

Dolo, Emmanual T. *Ethnic Tensions in Liberia's National Identity Crisis: Problems and Possibilities.* Cherry Hill, NJ: Africana Homestead Legacy Publishers, 2007.

Dudouet, Véronique. *Powering to Peace: Integrated Civil Resistance and Peacebuilding Strategies.* Washington, DC: International Center on Nonviolent Conflict, No. 1, 2017.

Ellis, Stephen. *The Destruction of Liberia and the Religious Dimension of an African Civil War,* 2nd edition. New York: New York University Press, 2006.

Ending Liberia's Second Civil War: Religious Women as Peacemakers. Berkley: Berkley Center for Religion, Peace, and World Affairs, 2013.

Galvanek, Janel B. *Pragmatism and Mistrust: The Interaction of Dispute Resolution Mechanisms in Liberia.* Berlin: Berghof Foundation, 2016.

Gbowee, Leymah Roberta. "Nobel Lecture." Oslo, December 10, 2011.

Meredith, Martin. *The State of Africa: A History of Fifty Years of Independence.* London: Simon & Shuster UK Ltd, 2005.

PBS *Backstage: Interview with Samuel Kofi Woods,* available at: **https://www.pbs.org/speaktruthtopower/b_wood.htm**

Press, Robert M. *Ripples of Hope: How Ordinary People Resist Oppression Without Violence.* Amsterdam University Press, 2015.

Sawyer, Amos. *Beyond Plunder: Toward Democratic Governance in Liberia.* Boulder: Lynne Rienner Publishers, 2005.

Schirch, Lisa and Manjrika Sewak. "The Role of Women in Peacebuilding." Global Partnership for the Prevention of Armed Conflict, 2005.

Schock, Kurt. "The Practice and Study of Civil resistance." *Journal of Peace Research* 50, no. 3 (2013): 277-289.

Schock, Kurt. "Social Movements, Nonviolent." In *The Blackwell Encyclopedia of Sociology,* edited by George Ritzer. Blackwell, Oxford, 2007, 4458-4463.

Sesay, M. A. "Bringing Peace to Liberia." *An International Review of Peace Initiative, Accord* 1, (1996). London: Conciliation Resources.

Shilue, James Suah. "Citizenship or 'Autochthony' in Post-Conflict Liberia?: The Perils and Challenges of Ethnic/Religious Connections Forged by War and History." *Journal of Religion, Conflict and Peace* 5, no. 1 and no. 2 (Fall 2011–Spring 2012).

Shilue, James Suah and Patricia Fagen. *Liberia: Links Between Peacebuilding, Conflict and Durable Solutions to Displacement.* Washington, DC: The Brookings Institution, 2014.

Sharp, Gene. *The Politics of Nonviolent Action (3 Vols.).* Boston: Porter Sargent, 1973.

Sulleabhain, A. *Leveraging Local Knowledge for Peacebuilding and Statebuilding.* 2015. Available at: **http://www.ipinst.org/2015/03/leveraging-local-knowledge-for-peacebuilding-and-statebuilding**

Tavaana. *Saying "Yes" to Peace. How the Women of Liberia Fought for Peace and Won*. Tavaana, available at: **https://tavaana.org/en/en/content/how-women-liberia-fought-peace-and-won**

Woods II, Samuel Kofi. "Civic Initiatives in the Peace Process." *An International Review of Peace Initiatives*, *Accord* 1, (1996). London: Conciliation Resources.

About the Authors

Janel B. Galvanek is the Head of the Sub-Saharan Africa Unit at the Berghof Foundation in Berlin, Germany, where she leads the Foundation's projects in Somalia, supporting mediation and dialogue initiatives among local communities in Hirshabelle and Galmudug States. Janel's professional focus includes insider mediation, infrastructures for peace, and engaging local actors in conflict transformation processes. On a volunteer basis, Janel is the director of Growing Tree Liberia, an NGO based in Germany that supports programs for disadvantaged children in Liberia. She holds a Master's degree in Peace Research and Security Policy from Hamburg University and an MA from Georgetown University in Washington, DC.

James Suah Shilue is Executive Director for Liberian NGO, Platform for Dialogue and Peace (P4DP) as of June 2012. Prior to occupying this position, he served as Liberia's Programme Coordinator for UN joint Programme/Interpeace initiative (2007–2012). He presently serves as chairman for CSOs Cluster on peacebuilding and national reconciliation. He is also an adjunct lecturer at the Department of Sociology and Anthropology at the University of Liberia. His professional areas of interest include, social research, post war reconstruction and development, rule of law, peacebuilding and conflict prevention, youth, women peace and security and human security. He has enormous experience working with national and international stakeholders to communicate complex findings into policy relevant action plans. He holds a master's degree in Social and Community Studies (De Montfort University, UK) and an MA in Development Studies (Institute of Social Studies, The Netherlands).